WILDERNESS SURVIVAL TIPS.

STEVEN SCHOOL

Wilderness survival tips

ISBN:1481071769
ISBN-13:9781481071765

DEDICATION

I dedicate this book to the conservation of our national wild lands, to the protection of the animals which dwell therein, to the non pollution of our oceans, and to the respect of our planet.

Wilderness survival tips

CONTENTS

	Acknowledgments	i
1	Experience.	1
2	Gold in the sierras	Pg #5
3	Mountain lion	Pg #6
4	Travelling	Pg #8
5	Bigfoot	Pg #9
6	Snow	Pg #11
7	Urban Preparedness	Pg #13

Wilderness survival tips

ACKNOWLEDGMENTS

I would like to acknowledge my grandmother, who raised me high in the sierra Nevada mountain range of northern California, which truly is god's country, and to the persons who took me on frequent excursions of hiking, hunting, camping, fishing, and gold mining deep in the secluded wilderness of California's gold country. You know who you are.

Wilderness survival tips

1 EXPERIENCE.

When I was growing up in the sierra Nevada mountains, my favorite activity was rugged wilderness hiking,

Exploring on foot, the rugged uninhabited sections of forested land, I always took my dogs with me, I also brought along a magnesium and flint fire starting tool, a pocket knife, a snake bite kit, a small water proof tube of matches, fish hooks and fishing line, as well as a canteen.

During my hiking experiences I came across a myriad of wild creatures at different times and places, including eagles, buzzards, all types of snakes, scorpions, spiders, biting stinging ants, bees, wasps, squirrels, lizards, rabbits, wild turkey, deer, bear, and mountain lions.

I found all kinds of old hard rock mine tunnels which had been built somewhere between 1840 and 1900. There were rusted ore carts, track, tailings piles, remnants of stamp mills where they processed the gold bearing ore which had been brought out of the tunnels with the ore carts. I came across many very old dilapidated wooden miners cabins from around the 1850 era.

I did in fact partially explore many of these tunnels, finding interesting artifacts. But I do not recommend this course of action to anyone else. If you come across such tunnels, stay out. They are prone to cave in, they contain areas of no oxygen, and they have sudden right angle turns going straight down into the earth, that you will never be able to climb back out of.

These tunnels have also been known to contain bear, mountain lions, rabid bats, rattle snakes, and old unstable ordnance such as nitroglycerin based TNT which is not to be touched, especially if it is sweating. It looks like an extra thick road flare filled with sawdust that has been impregnated with the liquid nitro. The old blasting caps were a wooden cap with a plug of gunpowder inside, and a fuse, the cap was intended to be slid onto the stick, and the fuse lit. the miners had giant hand drills, chisels and hammers, that they used to carve cylinders in the rock to place the sticks in. they were rugged fellows and this is why my grandmother always said, never mess with a hard rock miner.

In hiking rugged areas, it is actually very common to come across snakes, and I have in fact encountered many types of them. I one time decided to sit down next to a very bushy tree, I was there only for maybe a minute with my back to this tree, when I decided to look to my right. I immediately noticed a long light green colored snake slithering towards me very stealthily through the branches. The snake was coming towards my neck and had gotten very close. I do not know what type it was, but I assure you I got up and moved away very quickly. I have never seen another snake of that particular description since then, but I have encountered many others.

Upon vacationing to the southern states I have come across many snakes, as well as alligators while hiking. Eye opening indeed. An alligator can run very fast in a straight line, but they don't turn very well so if one is chasing you, run in a zigzag pattern putting some turns in your step. I actually saw a fisherman cast his line into a creek that was connected to a swamp, his lure penetrated the surface of the water and landed on the back of a submerged, fifteen foot long alligator which we had no idea was there. The disturbed gator came out of the water and chased the fisherman all the way back to his vehicle, I was far ahead of the fisherman. The police and fire department had to be called as this gator was chasing the mans vehicle, apparently wanting him for lunch. The gator was actually running down the highway towards a populated area. I suppose it is safe to assume, they can be aggressive.

Some types of venomous snakes can be aggressive too, such as the water moccasin, they have been known to sometimes actually come after a person. I have come across quite a few of these in my excursions.
One interesting snake I encountered in the state of Georgia was copper colored, its entire head and body were just like shiny copper except for its belly which was white.

Returning home, driving across country of course as I love road trips, I noticed something I would like to share with you. It was the state of Texas to be precise, I was driving along the highway at night, headed back to California. It was winter and being that Texas is such a large state it takes a good bit of time to cross it, therefore I was leaning a little heavy on the gas pedal, the roads were clear and dry, upon contacting a bridge I immediately began sliding as I had hit a sudden and unexpected patch of ice. This was an awakening experience and luckily I was able to slow down and correct my steering, before continuing on. A bridge will ice before a paved road will, so be alert of that, as I passed more bridges I saw other vehicles that hadn't been so lucky including a flipped motor home. The vehicle had literally fallen apart while rolling and was completely destroyed. Being an alert driver I feel completely safe behind the wheel, I never fly. If a plane crashes I can assure you I won't be the party which was aboard it.

Back to the mountains of California, I would like to share an event that occurred some few years ago. A turkey hunter was high up in a tree dressed in camouflage, far out into the wilderness and by himself with no dog as he wanted to retain stealth, for his hunt. He was in fact bow hunting, he was signaling with a turkey call hoping to attract his prey. Now a wild turkey is one of the favorite meals of the California mountain lion, and what followed the sound of the bleating was 3 lions, when these creatures arrived they discovered there was actually no turkey present, but they quickly determined the man in the tree would be a satisfactory meal instead.

The 3 lions decided that they, were going to eat this man, as they aggressively approached, he was forced to defend himself. He had to shoot one of the lions with an arrow. Upon seeing the demise, the other lions fled. So the moral of the story is, realize that if you are using an animal call in the wild, it may not be the animal you expect that arrives, and it may be looking for lunch.   This is also why I always take my dogs with me when hiking, a dog will alert you that the lion is approaching, dogs can easily smell these creatures. And while a lion will eat a large Rottweiler, if you have more than one dog there is a larger chance that they will chase the cat away, as long as they don't corner and attack it, forcing it to defend itself. If you encounter a cougar, do not turn your back on this creature, and do not run.

If you run from a predator such as this, it instinctively thinks that you are prey. Its natural instinct is to chase down a running mammal, and eat it. I read an article a few years back that a woman was running along a hiking trail in placer county California, near an area called the confluence which means two rivers coming together. I myself have hiked this trail many times.

In her particular case, one of these cats was perched on a ledge above the

5

trail, waiting for prey to come by. As this person was running past, the big cat pounced. The outcome was not good news. according to the news article, search parties found very little left. I myself never ran on this trail, I only walked and hiked, and all the times I went, luckily the trail was well populated with other hikers and people riding horses. The area itself is beautiful country, I myself enjoy panning for gold there, and jumping from high rocks, down into the pools of water below. As far as the gold is concerned there is still some there, but the place has been pretty well picked over for about the last 160 or more years, especially with the advent of the new pulse induction type of super gold detectors. There are however a few pockets left and as always, mother nature continues to make gold in the earth. There is another hiking area about 60 miles farther up highway 49 that is one of my favorites and still does have some gold left. It is the south fork of the yuba river at the old bridge which has been bypassed and is no longer in use, except as a public park. You must be careful of the under currents in the water here. I have actually encountered quite a few snakes here, but I have learned that if you pay attention you will see them in advance and can therefore simply avoid them altogether. Even when I came upon water moccasins in Georgia I learned to develop an eye for noticing these creatures. Moccasins like water, and they like to crawl up under anything they can to hide, such as rocks, a friend of mine pulls his rowboat up on shore and turns it upside down when not in use to keep the rain out of it. One day he went to use the boat and discovered an aggressive cotton mouth residing underneath. I can tell you from firsthand experience that they are nothing to play with. The California rattle snake likes to hide under rocks, it loves to sun itself on top of a warm rock on a sunny day, they will also burrow into the ground forming dens, and slither into caves. This snake is very common in the California mountains.

On a separate subject, once while I was camping I had the bad experience to be bitten by a large black widow spider while I was sleeping, I awoke and destroyed the hideous thing. There was no close medical attention around, luckily the bite was on my calf and not on my neck. My leg began swelling up and turned all sorts of colors such as black, blue, yellow, purple. The area of the bite was a raised lump, I could clearly see the two puncture marks. I began squeezing the lump and all kinds of pus was coming out. I heated some water as hot as I could possibly stand it, and began pouring it on the bite. I kept alternating squeeze out the pus, pour on the hot water, until no more pus would come out. I didn't feel quite right for a couple of days, but I was ok. If you get one of these bites it is important to seek medical attention immediately because people have actually died from these, But I also think where you get bitten, and how you treat it affects the outcome of the situation.

GOLD IN THE SIERRAS.

One of my favorite past times is gold mining, I find it very relaxing to be underwater with an oxygen hose on a hot summer day, vacuuming up sand and gravel into a dredge. This entails long hikes into remote wilderness areas, and packing in supplies and equipment. Being in seclusion far from civilization, and the cares of the world.

In 2007 I was invited to spend the summer dredging with my brother and a friend, on the north fork of the Yuba river. We packed in all of our equipment and set up our tents. I made an extra roof over my tent with a tarpaulin and rope in case of rain. We arranged a circle of rocks on the ground making a fire pit. We set up tiki torches. We had our German Rottweiler Rudy with us, he is an excellent watchdog and guarded our camp very well.

 In the mornings we would get up early, hike our way upstream, and fish for breakfast. Grilling up the fresh trout in our campfire. After breakfast we would wash up the dishes and head into the water for dredging. We encountered numerous rattles snakes, they were very common. We used sticks and rocks to neutralize the vipers, which was very effective. We spent the evenings barbecuing dinner over a fire, then relaxing under the stars, we quickly realized that bears were very common and they wanted to tear up our stuff. Our dog Rudy actually confronted one of them that had boldly walked right into our camp and helped itself to our ice chest. He charged at the bear snarling, growling, and snapping and chased it away. I was very impressed that a Rottweiler will protect and defend its owner, and its owners property against anything. The dog simply wasn't afraid to fight this bear that had walked into my camp. I since then decided to get an additional rottie and breed them. These two do an excellent job of protecting my house and property. I enjoyed spending that entire summer of 2007 camped out at the river, by the time it was over we had about two pounds of gold. Hikers passing by once in a while would stop and chat with us, telling us stories of their fishing and mining experiences, we made a couple new friends, although there weren't many that came by as far out in the wilderness as we were.

You can purchase bear repellant which is jumbo sized cans of maximum strength pepper spray, it launches a huge spray reaching as far as 30 feet away, it is not a bad idea to have a few cans of this.

MOUNTAIN LION

In the year of 1988 I had decided on the spur of the moment to go hiking with my dogs. This time, since my excursion was not pre planned, I did not bring anything at all with me. Just the clothes on my back and my dogs. I was hiking in a familiar area that I had been hiking for many years, this place is secluded and it was extremely rare, almost unheard of, to ever encounter another person here. Nonetheless I felt completely comfortable, and had not a care in the world. As I hiked along, my dogs became very excited, they began sniffing at the ground and then ran far ahead, completely out of sight, barking hysterically the whole way. I had no idea what this was about. They had sniffed a scent, and tried to follow the trail, but in the wrong direction. Something caused me to look to my left, and there, was a large California mountain lion. The lions eyes were deeply fixated on me, it was crouching which is what they do right before they pounce upon their prey. I turned and faced this animal, my eyes locked onto his. I stood up straight and tall, looking as large as possible. I growled a few swear words at this creature, I called it a few choice names because I thought this was my last day and that I would not be seeing home again. The cat hesitated when I faced it and made eye contact, they prefer to attack from above and behind, upon an unsuspecting victim. The big cat was perched on top of a wooden platform from an old water tank long since abandoned. The rotted weathered boards were kind of a grayish color from age, and falling apart. The water tank itself was rusting away.
I held my ground, the cat was about six feet above me, and about 10 feet to my left. Just the crouched animal began to spring, I heard the sound of my dogs crashing through the brush barking ferociously, this surprised the cougar and caused it to falter, it jumped to the ground in my direction, it stopped and looked at me for a split second, my gaze never leaving its eyes. Just then my dogs charged the creature, chasing it through the brush. The cat was lightning fast as it took off. I repeatedly tried calling my dogs back but they were intent on attacking, they had never seen one of these, but knew what to do. My dogs had disappeared into the woods. I reluctantly began the long walk home. I was worried about my pets, but they were nowhere to be found, and I didn't necessarily want to stay and play with the lion, or find out if its mate was nearby.

Luckily within a couple of hours, my dogs returned home unscratched. They were brothers.

I have heard since then, that if a lion is encountered, it is best to face the animal, stand up straight and make yourself appear as large as possible. Maintain eye contact at all times, and talk to the creature in a calm voice, they are not sure what to make of this large being which walks on two legs and makes strange sounds. Do not approach or act threatening, it may leave on its own, but if the cougar decides to attack, you must fight back with anything you have, rocks, sticks, knife, hands, feet, whatever. But if you turn and run then you are instinctively seen as prey. I further was advised later by a special forces soldier, that if an attacker pounces on you face to face and they are taking you to the ground, grab them with both hands and raise one knee towards their belly and they will impale themselves on your knee, knocking the wind out of them and leaving them stunned, giving you an opportunity to attack or to escape. I further was advised by another person later, you don't go into the woods without bringing something to protect yourself with , and I don't go without my dogs.

TRAVELLING.

If I am lost in the woods, the first thing I recommend is make a spear, about six feet long and two to three inches thick of hardwood. Use fire, and rocks to burnish and sharpen one end. Use the butt end to the ground as a walking stick. If you build a fire, build it against a boulder, it will reflect heat back at you, the smoke will travel up the side of the rock instead of in your face, and its less likely that the wind will put it out. Unless I know that civilization is uphill, it is easier and faster to walk downhill. Down leads to water, water leads to civilization. I travel in the day time. Keep your eyes and ears peeled for animals, snakes, smoke on the horizon, and sounds of civilization. At night I will keep a fire going all night in the hopes of warding off predators. If I am unable to gather enough wood, or get it lit, I will sleep in a tree and try not to attract animals with excessive sounds or movement. Many predators hunt at night, but some of them cannot climb a tree so I will just eliminate those, such as wild pigs for instance, coyotes, and wolves. If travelling in excessive heat, when I stop, I stop in shade, and preferably at a stream for fresh water. If a wild animal is encountered, hold the spear with both hands, with the point directed at the animal. Do not make threatening movements unless it attacks. keep your feet spread a little wider than shoulder width apart, with your knees slightly bent, maintaining good balance. If the beast comes at you, either ram the spear down its throat, or through its chest, whichever is easier, do it hard and fast, and don't let go of your weapon, keep it between you and your attacker at all times, so that this critter cannot come any closer, and if it tries, it will further impale itself on your weapon. If reduced to a knife, hold it by the handle, with the blade pointed down, sharp side facing away from you. With this you can punch, slash, or stick. A hand weapon you can use, point your finger straight and make it strong, thrust it deep into the eye socket. If this animal pounces on you from the front, and is taking you to the ground, grab it by the throat with both hands, raise your knee to its belly and let it impale itself as you go down, knocking the wind out of it, gouge the eye, if you have a knife, go between the ribs and finish it, or get up, retrieve your spear and use it. My belief is that if you are forced to fight in any situation, finish it, and do it quickly. Rocks make a nice smashing weapon, directed at the cranium. A handful of dirt or sand thrown in the eyes, or a pointy stick quickly picked up and jammed in the ear canal, the eye, or up the nostril. I also have been known to bite. A punch to the throat, a hammer fist to the head, a palm heel strike up under the chin.These are just a few defense ideas that come to mind. Lions usually pounce on their prey from above and behind, they do not like eye contact, so maintain it at all times. If you turn your back on a mountain lion, you might as well consider yourself lunch.

BIGFOOT ENCOUNTER.

In 1985, I was 15 years old, I lived high in the sierra Nevada mountains of northern California. Being a teen ager at the time, I sometimes was prone to sneak out in the middle of the night. One such occasion being summer time, I slipped out the window after midnight, I met up with a friend of mine who had also snuck out. We walked through the seemingly deserted woods in the moonlight, total distance about 10 or 12 miles round trip, as we were walking along at about 3:00 am we encountered a bigfoot.

This creature was about eight or nine feet tall, large, covered in dark matted strings that looked like a cross between hair and fur. It walked upright on two feet, a biped. We had crossed paths, and we were headed in different directions. The mammal stopped and looked at us, we stopped and looked at it, there being about 30 feet between us, and then we all three continued walking, while looking back at each other. These animals do not appear to be threatening or aggressive, they are nocturnal. They live in caves in secluded wilderness areas which are close to water.

These creatures are a hybrid cross of part humanoid, and part unknown primate species, possibly monkey, ape or Orangutan. It is not unheard of, that in jungle areas such as Africa, such couplings are rumored to sometimes occur, irregardless of the situation, I would say these animals were here in the cave man days. The word troglodyte comes to mind for some reason. I believe they were quite more common in prehistoric times that they are today, they are passive and reclusive. The Indians knew this creature and called it yeti. It is interesting that some persons over the years have found it humorous to pull prank bigfoot sightings by running around in a costume or leaving footprints. Some of those gags have actually been rather complex. But in myths, there is a spark of truth, that began the legend, otherwise myths wouldn't be interesting enough to remember over several centuries and different continents. Scientists are now taking more interest in the yeti, also known as sasquatch. It is rumored that a group of researchers from a university in California actually studied the animals after a gold miner tipped them about the location of a den found on a creek in Cal Ida, California. Cal Ida is a secluded wilderness area above Camptonville in the Sierra Nevada mountains. It is also rumored that a separate group of scientists may actually have a DNA sample which supposedly identifies the creature as being part human, and part unknown primate species, a hybrid cross.

I know that some of the Rambo type survival knives may seem kind of cheesy, but there are some that are better than others, and they contain enough to catch a fish, and start a fire. You can also stuff some of your own custom additions into the handle. Orion makes a blaze orange super loud, ear splitting signaling whistle. It has a cord to be worn as a necklace, the noise level of these is so piercing, you can get attention from quite a distance away. Marine supply stores are a good place to find these. The same company also makes a flat stainless steel signaling mirror that will fit perfectly in your back pocket.   I always keep a rugged back pack for hiking, its already got all my stuff in it, even t.p. all I have to throw in it, is bottled water and sandwiches. The knife I choose is the SOG, navy seal knife with kydex sheath. It is a sharp and durable fighting knife. Whatever wilderness gear you purchase, it doesn't do you any good if you left it at home and don't have it when you need it. With that being said, you might as well have a couple of Bic lighters among your primitive fire making tools and water proof matches.

SNOW.

Now if you are lost in the snow, there are few things that I would recommend, first of all if it is daytime, I would suggest to survey my particular surroundings, if I was planning to travel, I would plan on travelling downhill.

I would however, listen for sounds of civilization, I would also be alert for combustible materials that I could potentially stockpile for an all night fire.

If I were to find such a stockpile of combustible materials for an extended fire, I would plan on camping out there for a while, I would also plan on building a snow cave or similar type dwelling such as an igloo, to provide cover for myself from the weather, if nothing else it could serve as a windbreaker, to keep the icy cold bone chilling winds off of me, which would definitely increase the cold, especially at night.

If there were trees around which had green foliage covered branches that easily can be snapped off, I would consider breaking off a large assortment of these to line my snow cave with, sort of like blankets, below, and above me, so that I could crawl amidst this pile of foliage as if they were blankets per say, while the snow cave would serve to keep the icy cold bone chilling winds off of me so to speak.

If there were large boulders present, and if I had the ability to create and sustain a fire, I would build my fire against one or more of these boulders for several reasons, first of all, by building my fire against this supposed giant rock face, it would therefore reflect the heat of the fire, back towards me, also since the rock will absorb the heat, it may continue to project heat even after the fire goes out, another reason is that since the rock can deflect wind, said wind possibly having the ability to extinguish our fire, it may actually protect your heat source.

I also would take into consideration the fact that if there are snow burdened branches overhead, that this may not be the optimal place to create our fire, since the rising heat might cause the overhanging snow to fall and extinguish our fire.

Now if you have someone with you, then you should cuddle and try to keep each other warm. This is yet another example of why I want my rottweilers to be with me if I venture into the wilderness, animals are very intelligent, a dog can and will survive the snow, especially if there are a couple of them.

You can curl up between them, using their fur and body heat for warmth, also if any potential rescuers happen to come near you, the dogs will let you know. Since animals are so vastly intelligent, when daylight approaches, it might be best to just let the canines lead the way home, and you just follow them.

If you happen to encounter wild animals, it is your dog's natural instinct to protect you, and generally speaking, they seem to know just what to do. There are a few things that you should have in your pack if you are planning to head out into a snowy area, extra pairs of dry socks and gloves, a warm, thick ski mask, a metal cup to melt snow in, thereby creating an endless supply of drinking water. A flare gun with at least twenty flares, it would become very easy for search and rescue workers to find you, especially at night, with just a simple flare launcher gun.

You can also purchase survival blankets which fold up very small and don't take up much space at all, I would bring at least three or four of these, they are silver colored like a mirror, they are designed to hold in your body heat and to reflect it back towards you.

If you were to build an igloo out of snow, you could cover the floor with one of these blankets, and then wrap yourself up in a second one, you could also lay one of these things outside of your emergency shelter, on top of the snow, it can reflect sunlight and help to signal search parties to your location. People easily become snow blinded by the bright sunlight reflecting from snow, and then everything appears white which will tend to camouflage your survival shelter, you need something bright that really stands out for them to see, wrap the outside of your igloo with the blanket as a wind break, with the shiny side facing outwards, this is dual purpose, and keeping the icy winds off of you will help greatly.

URBAN DISASTER PREPAREDNESS.

It never hurts to be prepared for unexpected disasters at home, there are several things that you can do to increase your security by planning ahead for whatever may come. An underground shelter is a great idea, local home centers can order two thousand gallon plastic septic tanks, they can probably get larger ones as well. These are ideal to bury into the ground, since they are already shaped like a room, they are light weight and easy to move, they are water proof, and they have two large openings with lids built into the top, which can be used as emergency entrances, exits, and air shafts. You can also purchase large corrugated plastic drainage culvert pipes, bury these underground to create tunnels, or use them to connect two or more of these subterranean rooms together. You might pour a concrete slab on the ground over the shelter, and assemble a metal prefab carport roof on it, this will give you added protection and camouflage.

Assemble a shelving unit from your local home center inside one of these underground chambers, you can stock it with canned food, bottled water, a first aid kit, a small portable battery operated radio, blankets, instant coffee, extra clothes, ammunition, et cetera. A popular caliber of ammo for survivalist situations is twenty two, it is both inexpensive and light weight. You can store a large quantity of it in a small space, and if you have to travel, you can easily carry thousands of rounds in a back pack. It is also perfect for hunting small game to be used as food. I would also keep a good supply of wooden stick matches and candles, as well as battery operated lights with solar chargers to be used underground. I would not use the candles underground, but keep those inside your house with some kerosene lamps as well.

Install solar powered motion lights on your trees, and on the edges of your roofs. You can also purchase a battery powered driveway alarm with a remote motion sensor, this will let you know if anyone has invaded your perimeter with a loud siren set up indoors.

You can install steel security doors over the outside of your existing doors, these are designed to be fitted with an extra locking door knob, and a dead bolt.

Hire a local welder to fit your windows with security bars, they should be installed on the inside of your home for several reasons including the fact that they will not rust easily because they are not exposed to the weather, also because it makes it much harder for intruders to penetrate your home because they cannot access the bars to cut, dismantle, or remove these devices, they actually would have to break the window, and travel through the broken glass, before they can even touch the metal.

It is a good idea to have a security alarm system installed in your home, I myself also have installed fire alarms in every single room of my house, including two of them up in the attic, if there is a fire up there I want to know about it as soon as possible. You can also dig small trenches around your land, and using irrigation piping, install frost proof hose faucets. These devices stand about two feet tall, and they are protected against freeze breakage since the on off valve is actually located underground, it uses a long metal rod connected to the handle, which has an internal plunger on the other end. If an unexpected fire breaks out, it is wise to have these located in strategic positions around the outside of your home. I place a twenty foot hose on each of mine, and I use the larger three quarter inch garden hoses, since they will dispense more water than the standard sized hoses that most people will utilize in their gardens for watering lawns and plants.

Another good idea is to fence your property, I have installed a six foot high galvanized chain link fence all around the perimeter of my property, this will slow down intruders, especially if you have rottweilers patrolling inside the fence. I keep two of these dogs in my yard at all times, they can access my entire parcel of land, I also have a third Rottweiler inside my home at night, that I will let outside if the other two start barking.

I installed a metal locking mail box outside of my fence, it is large enough that postal workers can insert average sized packages into it, I used a four by four green pressure treated post, cemented into the ground to fasten it to, and it is clearly marked with reflective numbers and letters on three sides, as well as a private property, no trespassing sign on its post, there is a large oak tree directly behind this mailbox, and located just inside the fence. I placed a solar powered motion light on this tree, covering the mail box and the drive way, it is installed high enough on the tree that it cannot be reached without a ladder, I also placed a burglar alarm sign directly under this light.

If you're porches happen to be concrete slabs, which many of them are these days, when your railings need to be replaced, you can use concrete cinder blocks and fill them with concrete. This will last a long time, and it is relatively inexpensive. It can afford some protection against gun fire as well, especially if you replace the siding on your house with bricks. Now you quickly have a poor man's bunker.

When you are fencing your land, you can build six foot high cement cinder block walls along the back and sides of your property, it is a good idea to have the land surveyed first of course, to prevent encroaching upon and aggravating the neighbors. You can plant hedges that will grow above the height of this wall, which when neatly trimmed, look very nice, as well as affording a greater level of privacy, and preventing intruders from being able to climb over your wall. In the front yard you can build two foot high rectangular shaped planters out of red clay bricks and concrete, then install your galvanized chain link fence inside and at the forward edges of these planters. You can plant more privacy hedges at this location as well. At this point your home should have become very secure. Keep a boat with oars in the yard in case of emergency flooding, it does not need to have a motor. A simple rowboat, pedal boat, or canoe is fine. Keep a fire extinguisher, and a smoke alarm in the kitchen as well. It is a great idea to join a karate class, especially tae kwon do, or cardio kick boxing, this will keep you in great shape, and self defense ready.

This concludes my book on wilderness survival tips, and emergency disaster preparedness.

Other books by Steven School available on amazon.

How to make money.
Casino survival guide.
Grandmas delicious recipes.
Trophy wife.
Alchemy and the green lion.
Alchemy and the golden water.
Alchemy survival guide.
Alchemy and the peacocks tail.
Karate secrets revealed.